19·92

STRANGE PLANTS

Angela Royston

Heinemann Library
Des Plaines, Illinois

© 1999 Reed Educational & Professional Publishing
Published by Heinemann Library,
an imprint of Reed Educational & Professional Publishing,
1350 East Touhy Avenue, Suite 240 West
Des Plaines, IL 60018

Designed by AMR Ltd.
Printed and bound in Hong Kong/China by South China Printing Co. Ltd.
03 02 01 00 99
10 9 8 7 6 5 4 3 2 1
Library of Congress Cataloging-in-Publication Data

Royston, Angela.
        Strange plants / Angela Royston.
            p. cm. – (Plants)
        Includes bibliographical references (p.) and index.
        Summary : Discusses the behavior and adaptations of unusual plants,
    including strange flowers, ways of growing, storing water, feeding
    on insects, and more.
        ISBN 1-57572-829-X (lib. bdg.)
        1. Plants—Adaptation—Juvenile literature. 2. Plants—Juvenile
    literature. 3. Fungi—Juvenile literature. [1. Plants.]
        I. Title. II. Series: Plants (Des Plaines, Ill.)
        QK912.R69 1999
        581.4—dc21   98-44518
                                                              CIP
                                                               AC

Acknowledgments
The Publishers would like to thank the following for permission to reproduce photographs:
Ardea: I. Beames p. 14; Bruce Coleman: A. Compost p. 10, K. Taylor pp. 20, 21; Garden and
Wildlife Matters: pp. 4, 5, 6, 7, 8, 12, 15, 16, 19, 22, 23, 27, J. Burman p. 26, K. Gibson p. 18,
J. and I. Palmer p. 11, S. Shields p. 13; Chris Honeywell pp. 28, 29; Oxford Scientific Films:
D. Allan/Survival p. 9, W. Cheng p. 19, T. Middleton p. 24, K. Sandved p. 25.
Cover photograph: Gerald Cubitt, Bruce Coleman
Every effort has been made to contact copyright holders of any material reproduced in this book.
Any omissions will be rectified in subsequent printings if notice is given to the Publisher.

Any words appearing in bold, **like this**, are explained in the Glossary.

Contents

What Makes Plants Strange?

Some plants look strange. Others have a strange way of living. You will find out why these plants are strange in the book.

Strange plants are different from most
plants in some way. Most plants have
stems, leaves, and **flowers**. They have
roots that grow under the ground.

Strange Ways of Growing

Besides underground **roots**, mangrove trees have special roots that grow from the trunk down to the ground. These roots help to hold up the trees in the swamps where they grow.

All of these banyan trees grew from one trunk! Roots grow down from the branches into the ground. The upper parts of the roots become new trunks.

Storing Water

Plants need water to stay alive. Some plants that grow in dry places take in water when it rains and store it. This saguaro cactus stores water in its fat **stem**.

Baobab trees grow in dry places
in Africa. The trunk swells with
water during the rainy season. It
shrinks again during the long, dry
season.

Strange Flowers

A Rafflesia plant has one of the
biggest and worst smelling **flowers** in
the world! Its foul smell attracts flies
that spread its **pollen**.

The Titan Arum blooms once every six years, but its huge flower is worth the wait. It grows up to almost ten feet tall and then opens for only two days.

Stealing Food

Most plants make their own food, but some steal from others. The **roots** of this dodder plant grow into the **stems** of the heather and suck its food.

Can you see the mistletoe growing in this tree? It takes some food from the tree, but it also makes food in its own green leaves.

Living Together

Many plants live happily together. Orchids grow on trees in the **rainforest** and have long hanging **roots** that collect water from the air.

Lichen grows on stones and trees. It is really two plants that cannot survive without each other. One of these plants, called green alga, makes food for both of them.

Living with Ants

Some plants live with animals. Can
you see the ants on this strange **gall**?
The ants feed off the gall and stop
other insects from attacking the tree.

Ants also live inside the swollen **stem** of this ant plant. The ants feed on the plant and in exchange, they spread the tree's **seeds**.

Thorns and Stings

Many plants are eaten by insects and larger animals. Some plants protect themselves with thorns or stings. Look at the prickles on this thistle!

The leaves and **stems** of this nettle are covered with tiny stinging hairs. The hairs stick poison into any animal that brushes against them.

Catching Flies

Some plants eat insects! The red leaves of the Venus flytrap attract insects. But when one lands, the leaf snaps shut.

The leaf stays closed for about ten days while the plant oozes a powerful liquid that **digests** the insect.

Pitcher Plants

These pitcher plants are a deadly trap for insects. The inner walls are so slippery that once an insect crawls in, it cannot get out.

The insect drowns in the liquid that collects at the bottom of the plant. Its body slowly breaks up and is **digested** by the plant.

Plants That Hide

Can you see the plants hidden in these stones? These desert plants store water in their **stems**, but thirsty animals don't see them.

When it rains, the pebble plant
quickly bursts into **flower** and spreads
its **seeds** before the animals become
thirsty again.

Fantastic Fungi

Mushrooms and toadstools are **fungi.**
They are not really plants at all. They
can't make their own food. Instead,
they feed on living or dead things.

Most of the fungus is invisible. The
part you can see is called a fruiting
body because it produces **spores**.
Many fruiting bodies have weird
shapes and bright colors.

Growing Mold

Mold is a kind of **fungus**. You can grow
mold on bread in about one week.
Leave a slice of bread on a plate all day.

In the evening, pour half a cup of water over it and put it into a plastic bag. When the mold has grown, examine it through a magnifying glass.

Plant Map

A Strawberry Plant

flower

fruit

leaf

stem

roots

An Oak Tree

bark

leaves

roots

trunk

Glossary

digests	breaks up food into tiny pieces so they are small enough to pass into the body of a plant or animal
flower	the part of a plant that makes new **seeds**
fungus	a living thing that grows from a **spore** and is like a plant except that it feeds off other dead or living things
gall	a growth produced by a tree around eggs laid by an insect
pollen	grains containing male cells that are needed to make new **seeds**
rainforest	rainy place where many trees and plants grow together
roots	parts of a plant that take in water, usually from the soil
seed	a **seed** contains a tiny plant and a store of food before it begins to grow
spore	the cells from which a new fern, moss, or fungus begins to grow
stem	the part of a plant from which the leaves and **flowers** grow

Index

More Books to Read

Kite, L. Patricia. *Insect-Eating Plants.* Brookfield, CT: Millbrook Press, Inc. 1995. An older reader can help you with this book.

Lerner, Carol. *Cactus.* New York: William Morrow & Company, Inc. 1992.

Prevost. John F. *Orchids.* Minneapolis, MN: ABDO Publishing Company. 1996.

Stefoff, Rebecca. *Flytrap.* Tarrytown, NY: Marshall Cavendish. 1998.